Get Crafting for Your
GORGEOUS
GUINEA PIG

by Ruth Owen

BEARPORT
PUBLISHING

Minneapolis, Minnesota

CREATE!

Credits

Cover, © Igor Dutina/Shutterstock and © Jan Schneckenhaus/Shutterstock; 1, © Grigorita Ko/Shutterstock and © Ruby Tuesday Books; 3, © Ruby Tuesday Books and © Shutterstock; 4T, © Ruby Tuesday Books, © Grigorita Ko/Shutterstock, and © Jagodka/Shutterstock; 4C, © Ruby Tuesday Books; 4B, © Ruby Tuesday Books and © Africa Studio/Shutterstock; 5T, © Ruby Tuesday Books and © Dmytro Vietrov/Shutterstock; 5B, © Tatyana Vyc/Shutterstock; 6, © Ruby Tuesday Books, © Dmytro Vietrov/Shutterstock, and © Monica Butnaru/Shutterstock; 7, © Ruby Tuesday Books; 8, © Ruby Tuesday Books; 9T, © Ruby Tuesday Books; 9B, © Ruby Tuesday Books, © Grigorita Ko/Shutterstock, and © Jagodka/Shutterstock; 10TL, © Nataly Studio/Shutterstock; 10TR, © Nik Merkulov/Shutterstock; 10B, © Ruby Tuesday Books and © Igor Dutina/Ruby Tuesday Books; 11, © Ruby Tuesday Books; 12, © Ruby Tuesday Books; 13, © Ruby Tuesday Books; 14, © Ruby Tuesday Books and © Africa Studio/Shutterstock; 15, © Ruby Tuesday Books; 16, © Ruby Tuesday Books; 17T, © Ruby Tuesday Books; 17B, © Ruby Tuesday Books and © Valeri Potapova/Shutterstock; 18, © Ruby Tuesday Books and © Grigorita Ko/Shutterstock; 19T, © xstockerx/Shutterstock; 19B, © Ruby Tuesday Books; 20, © Ruby Tuesday Books; 21T, © Ruby Tuesday Books; 21B, © Ruby Tuesday Books and © Dmytro Vietrov/Shutterstock; 22TL, © In Green/Shutterstock; 22BL, © Pressmaster/Shutterstock; 22R, © Badon Hill Studio; 23, © BG-FOTO/Shutterstock.

Library of Congress Cataloging-in-Publication Data

Names: Owen, Ruth, 1967– author.
Title: Get crafting for your gorgeous guinea pig / by Ruth Owen.
Description: Create! books. | Minneapolis, Minnesota : Bearport Publishing
    Company, [2021] | Series: Playful pet projects | Includes
    bibliographical references and index.
Identifiers: LCCN 2020030858 (print) | LCCN 2020030859 (ebook) | ISBN
    9781647476625 (library binding) | ISBN 9781647476694 (ebook)
Subjects: LCSH: Handicraft. | Guinea pigs in art.
Classification: LCC TT157 .O8544 2021 (print) | LCC TT157 (ebook) | DDC
    745.5—dc23
LC record available at https://lccn.loc.gov/2020030858
LC ebook record available at https://lccn.loc.gov/2020030859

For more information, write to Bearport Publishing, 5357 Penn Avenue South, Minneapolis, MN 55419. Printed in the United States of America.

CONTENTS

GET CRAFTY WITH YOUR PIGGY

If you love taking care of your guinea pig and you enjoy getting creative, this is the book for you! Find four fantastic craft projects for your gorgeous guinea pig.

◁ Home Sweet Home
The wild relatives of guinea pigs are **prey** animals that hide from **predators**. Pet guinea pigs might feel the need to hide sometimes, too. This adorable piggy-sized camper van will give your pet a perfect hideaway.

Pet Snacks and Treats ▷
Guinea pigs are **herbivores**, which means they only eat plants. Build an **edible** train for your guinea pig made from tasty fresh veggies.

◁ Time to Play
Guinea pigs will get bored if they don't have things to do. Make this snuffle mat and sprinkle it with small pieces of food to give your guinea pig an exciting game of hide-and-snack!

Dress It Up

You are what you eat! Most guinea pigs will nibble on the yellow flowers of dandelions. So, make this cute costume for your little piggy and turn it into its favorite flowery treat.

Have Fun and Be Safe

Crafting for your best piggy pal can be lots of fun. But it's important that both you and your pet stay safe by following these top tips for careful crafting.

- Always get permission from an adult before making the projects in this book.

- Read the instructions carefully, and ask an adult for help if there's something you don't understand.

- Be careful when using scissors, and never let your guinea pig get close to them.

- Keep any paint or glue where your guinea pig can't sniff, lick, or touch it.

- When your projects are complete, recycle any extra paper, cardboard, or packaging. If you have leftover materials, keep them for a future project.

- Clean up when you've finished working.

- Remember! Some guinea pigs do well with gentle touching and attention. But others spend only a little time with their humans.

Never force your guinea pig to do something it seems unhappy to do.

PIGGY CAMPER VAN

Not only is this guinea pig camper van a good hideaway where your guinea pig can feel safe, it's also a quiet and cozy spot to sleep! A guinea pig is **active** both day and night, so it could use a cool place to take naps.

> If your guinea pig chews the van, remove it from your pet's space. Only give the van to your pet when you are there to keep watch.

You will need

- A rectangular cardboard box that's about twice the length and height of your guinea pig
- An adult helper
- Scissors
- A ruler
- A marker
- Tacky glue
- Paintbrushes
- Non-toxic paint

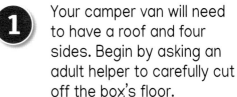

1 Your camper van will need to have a roof and four sides. Begin by asking an adult helper to carefully cut off the box's floor.

> Keep any cardboard scraps, as you will need them later.

2 Ask your helper to cut off one end of the box. This end will be where you make the front of the van.

3 Face the front of the box toward you. Draw a line across the top of the box that is about 2 inches (5 cm) from the front. Next, measure halfway up each side on the front edges of the box and make a mark. Use the marker and a ruler to connect the ends of the top line to the halfway marks.

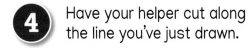 **4** Have your helper cut along the line you've just drawn.

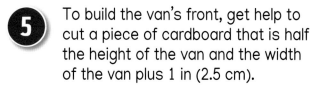 **5** To build the van's front, get help to cut a piece of cardboard that is half the height of the van and the width of the van plus 1 in (2.5 cm).

Glue here

6 Fold back a half an inch (2.5 cm) of cardboard along each shorter end to make flaps. Glue the flaps to the inside front of the van at the bottom.

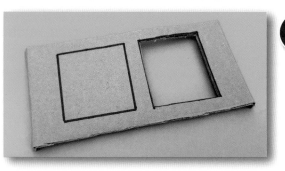

7 To make the van's windshield, measure and have your helper cut a piece of cardboard that is the height of the slanted edge and the width of the van plus 1 in (2.5 cm). Draw two windows onto this piece of cardboard, and have them cut out.

8 Fold back a half an inch (2.5 cm) of the cardboard on each side of the window part. Then, use the folded tabs to glue this section to the open space at the front of the van.

9 Ask your helper to cut a door in one side of the van that is big enough for your guinea pig to fit through.

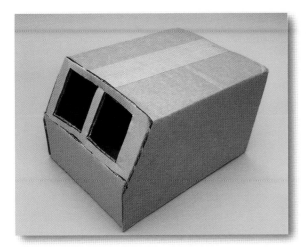

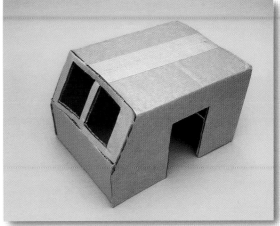

10 Your van is now ready to be painted. Decorate the van with windows, wheels, and lights.

Once all the paint is completely dry, your guinea pig can have fun in its new camper van.

TIME FOR A PIGGY ROAD TRIP!

THE VEGGIE EXPRESS

For a special treat, turn your piggy's veggies into a train that can be nibbled and munched. This recipe makes a train big enough for two guinea pigs to share.

You will need

- A cucumber that is straight and at least 8 in (20 cm) long
- 2 carrots
- 1 cherry tomato
- ½ cup chopped sweet peppers and mixed greens
- An adult helper
- A small kitchen knife
- A cutting board
- A ruler
- A teaspoon

Make sure you don't overfeed your guinea pig. Being overweight will make your best pal unhealthy and even sick.

1 Wash and dry the vegetables.

2 Ask an adult helper to use a sharp kitchen knife to cut your vegetables. To make the train's engine, cut a 3 in (7.5 cm) long piece from one end of the cucumber. Next, slicing lengthwise, cut off about a quarter of the piece of cucumber so the remaining thicker section lies flat.

3 Ask your helper to cut a 2 in (5 cm) piece from the main cucumber. This will be the **cab** for the train's engine.

Very carefully, they should cut a rectangular section of cucumber out of this piece.

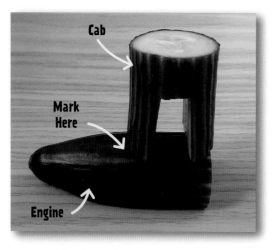

Cab

Mark
Here

Engine

4 Place the cab on top of the engine, lining up the back edges of the two pieces. Have your helper use the knife to mark where the cab ends. Remove the cab.

Very carefully, have your helper slice a thin layer of cucumber off the engine from the mark to the back of the engine. This will create a place for the cab to sit.

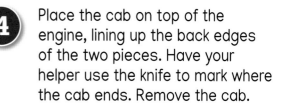

Remember, you can always cut off more. But if you cut off too much, you can't add it back on!

Hole
for the
chimney

5 At the front of the engine, have your helper cut and scoop a little hole to hold the engine's chimney. You should be able to fit the tip of your middle finger into the hole.

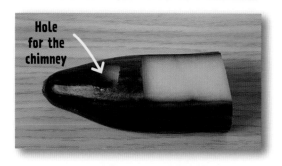

6 To make the wheels for the train, ask your helper to cut eight slices of carrot that are ½ in (1.25 cm) thick. Carefully have them slice a tiny part off the edge of each wheel, so it stands up and does not roll away!

Train car

7 To make the train car, your helper should cut a 3 in (7.6 cm) piece from the cucumber. Cutting lengthwise, carefully have them slice off about a quarter of the cucumber to reveal the inside **flesh**. Now, use a spoon to scoop out the soft flesh so this section can be used to hold vegetables.

8 Ask your helper to make a carrot chimney for the engine by cutting a piece of carrot until it is about 1 in (2.5 cm) tall and the thickness of a child's middle finger.

9 It's now time to build your veggie express in the place where your guinea pigs will enjoy their treat.

1. Stand the carrot chimney in the hole on the engine.

2. Place the cab on the engine.

3. Make a link between the engine and the train car with a cherry tomato.

4. Stand four carrot wheels, two on either side, against your engine, and four against the train car.

5. Finally, load the train with its cargo of chopped peppers and greens, and let your guinea pig start munching.

ALL ABOARD THE VEGGIE EXPRESS!

SNACK TIME SNUFFLE MAT

Make a toy that lets your piggy **forage,** or search, for tasty mouthfuls of food. This snuffle mat is the perfect place to hide food for your guinea pig to sniff out. The toy will keep your guinea pig active.

The snuffle mat can be used to feed treats or for your guinea pig's main meal. But make sure you do not overfeed your pet.

You will need
- A small rubber door mat with holes
- A ruler
- Scissors
- Soft, thick fabric

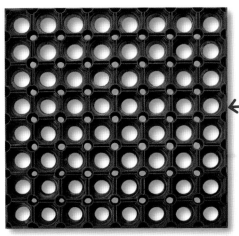

1 Begin by cutting your mat so that you have a grid that is eight holes wide and eight holes tall.

Most mats will be easy to cut. If you need help, ask an adult to cut the mat for you.

2 Carefully cut 56 strips of fabric that are 10 in (25 cm) long and 3 in (7.6 cm) wide.

You can use any thick, soft fabric, such as that from old sweatshirts, T-shirts, or even dish towels.

3 Tie your strips in vertical columns. Beginning in the top left-hand corner of your mat, thread a fabric strip down through the first hole (hole A) and up through the hole just below the first (hole B). Tightly tie the strip in a knot.

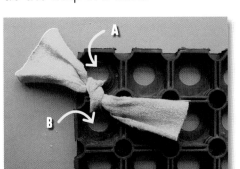

4 Next, thread a second strip down through hole B and up through the third hole (hole C). Tie it in a knot.

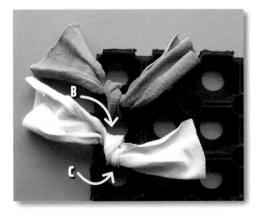

Front of mat

Back of mat

5 Keep tying strips until you get to the bottom of the column.

6 Repeat steps 3 through 5 until all the columns are completed.

7 Next, you will tie strips through the horizontal rows. Begin by carefully cutting 56 more strips of fabric.

8 Start in the top left hand corner again. Move the strips you've already tied out of the way to reveal the top row of holes.

9 Thread a strip through the first two holes in the top row, and tie in a knot. Then, keep tying strips all the way along the row.

Top row of holes

10 Repeat steps 8 and 9 until you have tied strips along all the rows. The finished snuffle mat should look like this.

Front of mat

Back of mat

11 Sprinkle a little of your guinea pig's food on the mat, and let your piggy get snuffling!

Always stay with your guinea pig when it's foraging on the snuffle mat. Pay attention to make sure it's not chewing the fabric or getting tangled in the fabric strips.

MMMMM . . .
DO I SMELL CARROT?

DELIGHTFUL DANDELION COSTUME

Some guinea pigs may eat from your hand, sit on your lap, or snuggle at your neck. Some may even be able to wear a costume and pose for some cute photos. Make this flowery costume for your pet.

You will need

- A helper
- A tape measure
- A green adult crew sock (a black, brown, or yellow sock will also look good)
- Scissors
- A marker
- Tracing paper
- A pencil
- Yellow felt
- A sewing pin
- A needle
- Thread (choose a color that's similar to the sock color)

18

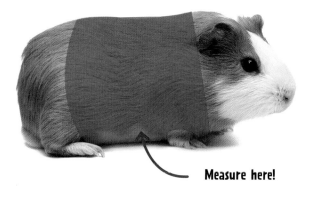

1 Begin by carefully measuring your guinea pig's body. Ask a helper to gently hold your guinea pig so it doesn't wiggle. Measure the animal from just behind its ears to just in front of its back legs.

Measure here!

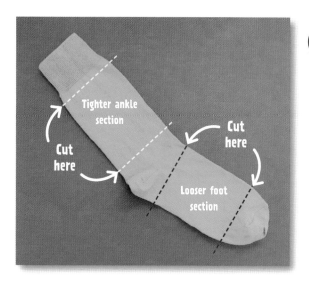

Tighter ankle section

Cut here

Cut here

Looser foot section

2 Cut a tube-shaped piece of sock that's the same length as the measurement you took in step 1.

You can use the tight ankle part of the sock or the looser foot section. Choose the part of the sock that will fit your guinea pig's body the best and will not be too tight.

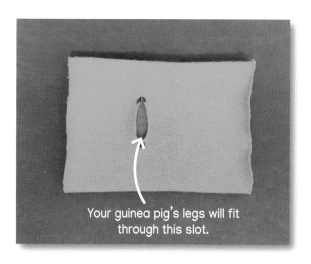

Your guinea pig's legs will fit through this slot.

3 Ask a helper to hold your guinea pig while you place the tube of sock against its tummy. Using a marker, make a small dot at each front leg. Now, cut a slot in the sock that connects the two dots.

4 To make the dandelion petals, use the tracing paper to trace the petal shape on this page. Cut it out.

You will need around 20 felt petals. This will depend on the size of your guinea pig.

5 Place the paper petal on the felt and carefully trace around it in pencil. Carefully cut out the felt petal. Repeat to make the rest of the petals.

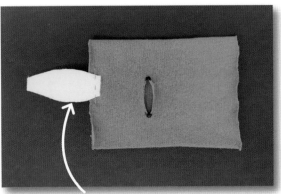

The base of the petal should be about 1/4 in (6 mm) below the edge of the sock.

6 Now, carefully pin a felt petal to the head end of the sock. Be sure to use the end near the leg holes!

Sew the petal to the edge of the sock, using about four or five small stitches. Remove the pin.

Always be careful when using pins. Be sure to keep the pin away from your guinea pig.

7 Next, pin a second petal beside the first and sew it into place. Repeat until you have a full circle of petals around the edge of the sock.

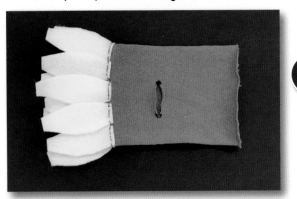

8 To make your piggy flower bloom extra big, add a second row of petals. Pin a felt petal to the sock in a space between two petals in the first row. Sew on the petal, and remove the pin.

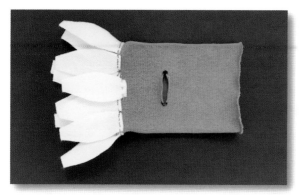

9 Repeat until you have sewn on a second row of petals.

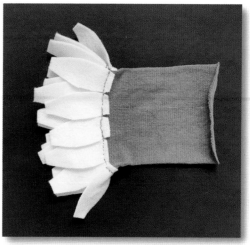

10 Making sure that there are no pins left in the costume, gently pull the sock part over your guinea pig's head. Carefully slide its front legs through the leg slot, and pull the sock down the body.

Only dress up your guinea pig for a few minutes, and stop if it seems upset. Never leave your delightful dandelion piggy alone when it is in the costume.

JUST GORGEOUS!

TOPS TIPS FOR A HEALTHY, HAPPY GUINEA PIG!

Being a **responsible** guinea pig owner is all about keeping your pet healthy and happy. Here are 10 tips to help you take care of your guinea pig.

1. Pigs are very **sociable** animals. They need attention every day!

2. Guinea pigs do best when they live with their own kind. Try to keep guinea pigs in pairs.

3. Cats and dogs may seem friendly to your guinea pig, but never leave your guinea pig alone with these animals.

4. When you pick up your guinea pig, always hold it with two hands and support its legs.

5. Ask your vet for advice on the best foods to feed your guinea pig and how much to give it.

6. Remove any uneaten food from your piggy's space and throw it away. Old food can become moldy and make your pet sick.

7. Clean and refill your guinea pig's water bottle every day.

8. Each day, remove any **droppings** or wet bedding from your guinea pig's space.

9. You may see your pig eating poop straight from its bottom. This is normal! Guinea pigs have special poop. Eating it helps your pet get more goodness from its food.

10. A guinea pig may live for around five or six years. Before becoming a guinea pig parent, make sure you are ready to care for your little friend for that whole time.

GLOSSARY

active moving around a lot and getting plenty of exercise

cab the front part of a train or truck where the driver sits

droppings animal poop that look like little balls

edible able to be eaten

flesh the soft, inside part of a fruit or vegetable

forage to look for food in the wild

herbivores animals that eat only plants

predators animals that hunt and eat other animals

prey animals that are hunted and eaten by other animals

responsible caring, trustworthy, and in charge

sociable likely to do well when interacting with others

INDEX

READ MORE

Fields, Hannah. *Is a Guinea Pig a Good Pet for Me? (The Best Pet for Me)*. New York: PowerKids Press, 2020.

Jacobs, Pat. *Guinea Pig Pals (Pet Pals)*. New York: Crabtree Publishing, 2018.

LEARN MORE ONLINE

1. Go to **www.factsurfer.com**

2. Enter "**Crafting Guinea Pig**" into the search box.

3. Click on the cover of this book to see a list of websites.

ABOUT THE AUTHOR

Ruth Owen has been developing and writing children's books for more than 10 years. She lives in Cornwall, England, just minutes from the ocean. Ruth loves all animals—wild and pets. Her favorite thing about guinea pigs is the whistling, squeaking noises they make to each other and their humans!